Bigger Than Hip Hop

7 Questions for Effectively Reaching Young Adults in Ministry

By: Ron Bell Jr., M.A.

Bigger Than Hip Hop
7 Questions for Effectively Reaching Young Adults in Ministry
Copyright © 2014
Published by: RonaldBellJrMinistries
www.RonaldBellJr.com
ISBN 13: 9780615985985
ISBN 10: 061598598X

All rights reserved. No part of this publication may be reproduced, stored in a retrieval system, or transmitted in any form or by any means-electronic, mechanical, photocopying, recording, or otherwise without the prior written permission of the author.

To

My Wife, thank you for being my theme song, a melody that never ceases to motivate me toward our destiny.

Contents

- Introduction...1
- Chapter 1: Motivations...3
- Chapter 1: Group Responses..............................7
- Chapter 1: Notes Section....................................8
- Chapter 2: Support...9
- Chapter 2: Group Responses............................13
- Chapter 2: Notes Section..................................14
- Chapter 3: What's Missing................................15
- Chapter 3: Group Responses............................19
- Chapter 3: Notes Section..................................20
- Chapter 4: Image..21
- Chapter 4: Group Responses............................25
- Chapter 4: Notes Section..................................26
- Chapter 5: Worldview..27
- Chapter 5: Group Responses............................31
- Chapter 5: Notes Section..................................32
- Chapter 6: Attraction...33
- Chapter 6: Group Responses............................37
- Chapter 6: Notes Section..................................38
- Chapter 7: First Steps..39
- Chapter 7: Group Responses............................43
- Chapter 7: Notes Section..................................44
- Chapter 8: The Point of it All............................45
- Appendix A...47
- Appendix B...51

Introduction

Introduction

When I graduated from seminary I was privileged to get a position in ministry quickly. I was hired to work with the Peninsula-Delaware Conference of the United Methodist Church as Director of Strengthening the Black Churches and Director of Congregational Development. That's a long sentence that basically means I got a job on the lower eastern shore of Maryland, helping United Methodist churches start new ministries. The conference consisted of over 400 hundred churches; my first year in the position was spent visiting with as many pastors and churches, among that 400, as possible.

The more churches and pastors I visited, the more I began to see several themes develop. For one thing, I noticed an absence. Many of these churches were filled to capacity, with only two generational groups: grandmothers and their grandchildren. The people in the congregations were either over the age of 55 or under the age of 15. The pews were generally devoid of young adults in the age range 20-40 years old. This missing generation interests me because it is the generation of which I am a member. In conferring with several colleagues from other denominations and churches, they concurred regarding the general absence of that same generational group. So, the question presented itself: "What's happened to the hip-hop generation, and what kinds of ministries and churches need to be developed to get them engaged in the life of the church again?".

Why Hip Hop and not Rap:

The term Hip Hop Generation, as a grouping, is specific. What I saw missing, and what I could identify with were those people born between 1975-1995. This era, specifically for many urban youth, was marked as the birth and subsequent explosion of Hip Hop. Hip Hop can be defined in many ways, but for the purposes of this book it is loosely defined as a brand and a self-expression that is focused on freedom and creativity, lived through multiple outlets such as music, art, culture, and social causes. Hip Hop is a way of life. It is the individuals defining themselves and lovingly expressing his or her new-found definition of self through as many means as possible.

What separates Hip Hop from rap is that rap is limited in its scope. Rap is the ability to merge rhythm and words; it is the marriage of ideas and sound. While rap is a beautiful and valid expression of self, it's just one expression out of many. Hip Hop is much broader; when Hip Hop burst on to the scene in the late 70's, it did so as a cultural shift, and rap followed Hip Hop's entrance into the American scene as a form of expression.

My Process:

I wanted to get a fresh perspective on the Hip Hop generation, their needs, ideas and what the church and/or potentially new ministries could do in order to engage this generation. In order to do this, I developed 7 questions that are presented in the following chapters. Participants were carefully selected and were required to possess specific qualities. First, they had to be born between 1975-1995. If I was going to get a grip on the needs and thoughts of this generation I needed to include them in the research. The second quality I looked for was that the individual needed to have a role in ministry. I wanted to make sure that the people who would be offering their wisdom did so having a fuller knowledge of the church, current ministry offerings and existing challenges. Lastly, I wanted to include people who expressed themselves through ministry using their gifts and talents. This quality was specifically designed to attract true Hip Hop generational people. Given these parameters, I ended up interviewing 25 young adults. These young adults came from all across the nation and included both those from denominational backgrounds as well as those from non-denominational settings. So, with those parameters…

Here we go!

Motivations

(age 32)

"Mediocrity should never be in your vocabulary."

-Pastor Okey Nwaneri, United States Air Force Chaplin.

Chapter 1

Motivations

Isaiah 6:8
Also I heard the voice of the Lord, saying, whom shall I send, and who will go for us? Then said I, Here am I; send me. KJV

The first question posed to the group of 25 young adults was:

What motivates you to do what you do?

INSIGHT

One of the unique factors of the Hip Hop generation is the overwhelming importance of motivation. Motivation, for the purposes of this book, is defined as a compelling spark that attracts both attention and a sense of purpose. The word "motivate" comes from an old French word, motif, meaning drive, will, or to bring something forward. What the Hip Hop generation is looking for is exactly that; a spark that drives them to purposeful action.

The importance of this factor must not be downplayed. If this generation of people is going to seriously engage in any ministry in the church or outreach event, there must be something in the construction of the event that motivates them. This needs to be considered in tandem with the needs of other generational groups. For example, the GI generation: those born between 1900-1924, acts primarily out of a sense of obligation. That generation of people does what's right; simply being told that it is the right thing to do, which is enough for them to conform to tradition without question.

Where you begin to see this critically unfold is in application of church doctrine. The Hip Hop generation is quick to question the significance of traditions, rules and structure. This questioning comes from that same place of seeking a motivating factor. Their curiosity and questioning should not be confused with abject rebellion. They are simply searching for meaning, and if possible, streamlining.

STRATEGY

To engage this group, there are several things that can be done.

1: Tell the Story.

This group needs to hear the story; the mere fact that something is "tradition" or "has always been done that way" is insignificant. This group needs to know where the "tradition" came from, what it means now, and why it's still relevant.

2: Get on at the ground floor.

If new ministries, new studies, or evangelistic opportunities are going to be successful, this group has to be in on the ground floor. This generational group needs to feel that not only their voices, but their efforts are an invaluable piece of the success of what's coming and what's happening.

3: Keep it short and sweet.

While this generational group is full of energy and ideas, they are short on patience and endurance. This group is not interested in a 36 week study or 3 month campaign. This group needs to see short goals and quick wins. What this means for those planning ministries is that there needs to be a staggered or phased design. Each completion of a stage needs to be celebrated and acknowledged. This will keep the interest of this generation.

APPLICATION

Weeks before we were to conclude our coat drive at Arise, from the pulpit I shared with the congregation an experience I had in my early twenties of being without electricity and having to bundle up with coats and blankets at night to stay warm. I then shared with the group a story about my favorite overcoat; one I bought and wore for years- so much so that the pockets had no bottoms and the original buttons had long since been lost. I informed the group that as the coat drive was coming to a close, I was going to donate that overcoat and was looking for at least 30 coats from them to be alongside it. As a result of sharing the story with them, including them in the process, and giving them short and achievable goals, the congregation experienced a motivation that compelled them to become newly invested in what would have normally been a routinely pedestrian coat drive. They were so motivated that at the conclusion of the coat drive, our congregation of 80 people donated 14 super-sized lawn-and-leaf bags full of coats, sweaters, pants and even blankets.

Group Responses to question 1:

What motivates you to do what you do?

- ✓ My Love for changing things around me
- ✓ My Daughter
- ✓ Something inside of me; a drive to help others
- ✓ A feeling that something needs to be done
- ✓ Putting a smile on people's faces
- ✓ Knowing the position I was in when I was little and needed someone
- ✓ Jesus
- ✓ Witnessing human suffering
- ✓ My Love and commitment to God
- ✓ My Love for my family
- ✓ The satisfaction of seeing God use my pain to encourage others
- ✓ My desire to be an instrument of God
- ✓ The spirit of God within me

Notes Section

What Motivates You?

_____
_____
_____
_____
_____
_____
_____
_____
_____

Ask a young adult what motivates them. What similarities do you hear and what differences do you see in your response?

_____
_____
_____
_____
_____

Support

(age 32)

"Young adult ministry is challenging. However, the reward of seeing a life changed is incomparable."
-Missionary and Pastor Travis Dunlap

Chapter 2

Support

> *1 Kings 19 16-18*
> *"Also you shall anoint Jehu the son of Nimshiasking over Israel. And Elisha the son of Shaphat of Abel Meholah you shall anoint as prophet in your place. It shall be that whoever escapes the sword of Hazael, Jehu will kill; and whoever escapes the sword of Jehu, Elisha will kill. Yet I have reserved seven thousand in Israel, all whose knees have not bowed to Baal, and every mouth that has not kissed him."*

The second question I asked the group was:

What kind of support/mentoring system would be helpful for you in ministry and life?

INSIGHT

Do you remember that scene in The Wizard of Oz when the characters finally realized that there was a regular man behind the curtain operating the giant head machine? That disconnect from intentional vulnerability and perceptional grandeur is something the Hip Hop generation lives on a daily basis. It is comparable to that statement every side view mirror carries: "Objects are closer than they appear." The truth is, this generation of young adults is in dire need of support and mentoring but don't have the language to ask for it. As a result, they attempt to go their own way, protecting their creativity and space and putting on airs while, at the same time, silently calling out for help.

This disconnect is visible in two specific areas: interpersonal relationship dynamics and financial wisdom/stewardship. Take a look around you. How many Hip Hop generational persons do you know who are struggling with how to be effective husbands, wives, or parents...how many do you know who are drowning under the burden of student loans, credit card debt, high interest car payments and bad mortgages?

While this is a book primarily focused on creating new and effective ministries by empowering the Hip Hop generation to take more of a critical position in the church, it is impossible to put together any sort of structure without engaging and honestly caring for the "real life" needs of this generation. There are critical pieces of wisdom that this generation is missing; knowing how this came to be and why they are missing this wisdom is less important than the prevailing question: How can we support them now?

STRATEGY

To engage this group, there are several things that can be done:

1: Get over it.

This generational group is not going to come to you asking for wisdom or advice. This does not mean that they are not welcoming or in desperate need of wisdom. If you feel called to mentor or support this generation, just do it. Take charge; be consistent, non-judgmental and available. Those characteristics are invaluable and will open more doors of vulnerability and realness than you can imagine.

2: Leave the Bible at Home

This generation isn't looking for more scriptures or sermons. What this generation needs is to hear your testimony. They need to know that you were once where they are. They need to know that they are not the first generation to have children outside of marriage, or the first generation to struggle with issues around sexuality. To effectively mentor and support this generation you will need to be transparent, vulnerable and honest.

3: Don't Fake It

Don't hold back. This generation likes to hear the raw uncut version. To make a real impact in their lives as mentors you will have to be real. This generation has been inundated with authority figures who have failed them; national, political and even religious persons who have crumpled under exposed scandal. As a result, the Hip Hop generation is cautious, yet actively listening for hints of truth.

Application

When we first started Arise, we started in the fellowship hall of an older United Methodist Church, meeting only on Friday nights. Every week for almost eight months, we would have to unload and cart in equipment, set up chairs, and construct the stage; then, after worship,we had to tear everything down and load it back up in our vehicles, only to repeat the process for the next worship service. What I discovered was that the more I showed up to help with a non-judgmental, transparent and "real" attitude, the more impact I had on this groups of guys. Just by being present and engaging with them in the work that they were doing for the church, I was able to impact their lives, pray for their relationships and give wisdom and guidance to their lives. We would have discussions while unfolding chairs that could rival any "Dr. Phil moment". Questions would be asked during those times that I'm certain had never posed publically to anyone before. But, because they felt heard, valued and safe, they were able to unpack a lot of issues that were weighing heavily on their hearts. In turn, they feel that you care, and that you are genuinely listening to them.

Group responses to question 2:

What kind of support/mentoring system would be helpful for you in ministry and life?

- ✓ I could use a pastor who is consistent in support
- ✓ Someone who gives back to those that dream
- ✓ A ministry that intentionally develops leaders and talks about real issues
- ✓ New Christians being linked within the congregation like a buddy system
- ✓ Older women who were able to admit that life gets messy
- ✓ An old, retired lady with a keenly sharp mind and great sense of humor
- ✓ Meeting once a month with my pastor
- ✓ Having someone older give me advice and coach me
- ✓ Having seasoned, creative leaders share their experiences
- ✓ Financial support
- ✓ Simply being available when needed without having to go through hoops
- ✓ Someone willing to impart what they have learned in me

Notes Section

Who has supported you in your past and what did that support look like?

_____
_____
_____
_____
_____
_____

Ask the young adults around you, what kind of support do they need?

_____
_____
_____
_____
_____
_____
_____
_____

What's Missing

(age 31)

"If I can get others to see that the gifts in their hands can part the waters of adversity, depression, lack, and hopelessness...I've done my job as a dream coach to a nation of dream chasers."

-Dr. Eboni M Bell

Chapter 3

What's Missing

Scripture:
Acts 2 46-48
[46] Every day they continued to meet together in the temple courts. They broke bread in their homes and ate together with glad and sincere hearts, [47] praising God and enjoying the favor of all the people. And the Lord added to their number daily those who were being saved.

Question:

What is the church missing that would benefit you and your friends?

INSIGHT

The church is missing relevance. One of my favorite Bible stories is that of David and Goliath. I love the story, because on many levels, it's really a story about relevance. The narrative plays out that one giant (Goliath) is able to paralyze a whole army because he has convinced them that he (Goliath) is more relevant than their leadership (Saul) and headship (God). Goliath uses fear to establish relevance, and up until the entrance of David, he is successful. Relevance is critical.

In order to be relevant, much like Goliath and exactly like David, we have to speak to the reality of the situation, and call it like it is. It is impossible to be relevant and ignore reality- or worse, purposely misinterpret facts to benefit self. How does this play out in the church?

Relevance looks like:	Creating single mom ministries.
Irrelevance looks like:	The absence of changing stations, licensed daycare/youth staff and amenities.
Relevance looks like:	Church members creating or joining a citywide basketball or football league.
Irrelevance looks like:	Ignoring the high crime rate of youth in your city or complaining that the children have nothing to do.
Relevance looks like:	Inviting financial institutions to teach ongoing financial health sessions at your church.
Irrelevance looks like:	Pretending that dwindling offerings will magically begin to grow if you preach harder.

Strategy:

To engage: use the Stop, Drop and Roll principle.

1: Stop

When someone is on fire, wisdom tells us that the first thing they should do is stop moving. For us, this means taking an assessment on the actual needs of this generational group. This can be accomplished by asking them what their needs are, surveying them, and by observing their patterns of behavior. For example, are you seeing less and less men coming to your church, but more women and kids in the pews? Are you hearing dialogue and questions about local political events or major community needs such as education, jobs or crime? The more you find out about what is really going on in your church members' daily lives, the greater impact and more relevance you will be able to have.

2: Drop

Essentially, there are things that we are doing now in our ministry that serves us no purpose in connecting and relating to the Hip Hop generation. These are things we can drop because of irrelevance. In order to figure this out, ask the Hip Hop generational group to assess and rate your ministry- and be ready and willing to hear their responses.

3: Roll

Every church is full of people with specific skills and gifts. Success is the byproduct of empowering passionate people to construct a clear purpose. When you determine what gifts are "in the house" and match them with the needs you have, you will find that you will be able to roll forward.

Application

We moved Arise into a new building in the city of Wilmington, Delaware in August of 2013; by the end of that year, in the city of Wilmington there had been over 156 shootings, many ending in death. As a result, relevance for us looked like creating a Say No More campaign (a social media tool focused on uniting as many people as possible around ending violence), meeting as a group to pray for the city, meeting with elected officials to discuss constructing safe zones and places for our youth to go, and partnering with other churches interested in making a real impact on our city.

Group responses to question 3:

What is the church missing that would benefit you and your friends?

- ✓ Balance and true examples of integrity
- ✓ Productive men!! Godly men.
- ✓ A Church that actually speaks truth
- ✓ More emphasis on social justice
- ✓ Honesty and a willingness to discuss difficult issues
- ✓ Activities to do outside the church, social gatherings
- ✓ A group of men to compel my husband to participate
- ✓ A very involved singles ministry
- ✓ Stronger community
- ✓ An open mind and understanding that God can move in different ways
- ✓ Informal church gatherings
- ✓ A purpose for worship
- ✓ Mentors and better outreach ministries
- ✓ True fellowship
- ✓ Love
- ✓ Balance

Notes Section

If you could redesign church the way you wanted, what would you add?

Ask 3 young adults what they see missing in the church. How do your answers and their answers line up? Or, do they line up?

Image

(age 31)

"The experience of being deeply loved by God fills me with a desire, like "a fire shut up in my bones," to see others in my generation experience that healing and unconditional love" --Rev. Hannah Bonner

Chapter 4

Image

Scripture:
Matthew 3 4-7
[4] John's clothes were made of camel's hair, and he had a leather belt around his waist. His food was locusts and wild honey. [5] People went out to him from Jerusalem and all Judea and the whole region of the Jordan. [6] Confessing their sins, they were baptized by him in the Jordan River.

Question:

What do you look for in a pastor, church, or worship service?

INSIGHT

I've owned several vehicles; my favorite, thus far, was a 1991 Jeep Cherokee. It was a limited edition model with all the bells and whistles. The only downside was that when I bought it, it was already well over ten years old and had over two hundred thousand miles on it. It was a beautiful vehicle, but riddled with constant engine issues, structural damage and an unimaginable amount of underbody rust. In short, it was beautiful, but not drivable. As a result, I found that the city bus was more reliable than my cherished Jeep Cherokee.

Many in the Hip Hop generation view pastors and church the same as my Jeep Cherokee. They can be beautiful on the outside, with all the bells and whistles, all the latest innovations, the biggest and best choirs, flamboyant and attractive pastors but…non-drivable. What is important to this generation isn't the flash- it's the substance. The question the Hip Hop generation has for the church is the same that I had for my Jeep….can it take me where I need to go?

What the generation is looking for are preachers who teach, not those who shout; ministries that empower, not those who drain time; and resources and churches who focus outwardly, not those who only want to fill pews.

STRATEGY

1: Increase your Visibility

Be visible. Find out where your members hang out, and show up. Choose local businesses around your church to establish relationships with, and invite your members to hang out with you in those places. The key is to let them see you interact with others in a non-church, "normal" way. I may be a pastor, but I'm also a husband, a dad, an entrepreneur, and a student. The more we share those elements of ourselves, the more effective we are in impacting the lives of those in our church.

2: Deliberate

(For Pastors) Have you ever watched yourself preach? Seriously, have you really watched and listened to yourself? Record one of your sermons, watch it with the sound on mute and just observe your body language; then, ask yourself what you're communicating. Next, watch it again with the sound turned up and try to take notes based solely off what comes out of your mouth. I'm betting that once you do this a couple of times, you will begin to see areas that could use growth.

3: Obtain Feedback

Create a culture in your church that honors feedback. Consistently, ask visitors and members their opinion on worship and the preaching. In preaching, acknowledge changes that have been made and give credit to those who suggested it. The more people feel that their voice is being heard; the more effective you are able to be.

Application

When we started Arise, my son was just a year old. In fact, his birthday was our launch day, 9/26/2012. As a result, I quickly had to dismiss some of the traditional notions of church I'd grown up with. For example, there was no reason to get dressed up to come to church, since my son was inevitably going to spit up (or worse) on me, at some point during the worship experience. Also, rules of no food in the sanctuary were out because this kid needed his snacks. Lastly, I knew that he was going to cry and would probably need changing so…you guessed it; we had changing stations in the back of the sanctuary. In fact, if you watch some of the early worship experiences at Arise online, you will hear several kids in the background at different times crying, or see them running across the screen. A year into Arise, we had a number of newborns, toddlers and young kids running around. This dynamic completely helped reframe ministry for us, and as a result, drew in young families, single moms and older adults into the ministry; because they saw us being real, and they felt comfortable making Arise their home church.

Group responses to question 4:

What do you look for in a Pastor, Church or Worship Service?

- ✓ Humility in pastors
- ✓ In a pastor, true words from the spirit
- ✓ A leader with a shepherd's heart
- ✓ A pastor who is a teacher at heart
- ✓ Honesty, sincerity and strong compassionate leadership
- ✓ Anointing and authenticity in pastors
- ✓ Love
- ✓ People passionate about getting into the presence of God
- ✓ Honest people with honest struggles
- ✓ Pastors to lead, teach, encourage, fellowship
- ✓ Preachers who can preach!
- ✓ Transparency, balance, purity
- ✓ Diversity of cultures

Notes Section

Who is your favorite celebrity, and what makes that person stand out to you?

How do those qualities compare to what you look for in a pastor?

Worldview

(age 40)

"Everything that I am, and all that I hope to be is because of God. Without him, I am nothing." -Pastor Kevin Hughes

Chapter 5

Worldview

Scripture:
Habakkuk 2:2
And the LORD answered me: "Write the vision; make it plain on tablets, so he may run who reads it.

Question:

What do you hear from those around you regarding their needs in terms of ministry, and in general?

INSIGHT

As a member of the Hip Hop generation, I want to use my own story as an example. I'm a husband, father, pastor, author, business owner, employer, musician, and student, and I love to read in my spare time. In short, I'm busy. My daily life moves at 90 miles an hour. As a result, traditional ways of doing ministry are generally either too slow and consuming for my life style, or they just can't keep pace with the rate at which my life is moving.

The reality is, many in the Hip Hop generation live life at that same speed. Between working several taxing jobs, launching their own personal businesses, expressing their creativity through arts or sports, and juggling family responsibility with educational desires, this generation is on the go. What the church is missing is how to relate to such a pace.

Because of the speed at which this generation moves, what they are in need of is ministry that's streamlined. They need meetings and study groups that can be accessed online or by phone (archived so that they can be accessed at convenience) instead of in person, and worship experiences that focus on powerful encounters with Christ and less on religious function or laborious order of service. This generation needs church to move at their speed. They need mentors and disciple makers who can check in via text, meet for coffee during lunch and then head back to work. They need powerful simplicity.

Remember the first cell phone, remember how big and heavy it was and the bag it came in; remember how hard it was to even purchase and access it. Now think about your current cell phone and its lightness, its functionality, its ease at access. It's powerful, but simple. Church needs to follow that same model.

STRATEGY

1: Repaint the Walls

The church as a whole does some great work, specifically when it comes to reaching out to the community. The challenge becomes thinking of ways to repaint the work that's already being done so that it is attractive and appealing to the Hip Hop generation. This can be done by looking at three areas: 1, the name of the ministry, 2, the function and access of the ministry and 3, the focus of the ministry. Example: Instead of having a youth ministry, try creating a step team that meets weekly and visits local colleges throughout the semester to meet with college fraternity and sororities for insight and mentoring.

2: Ditch the Keys

There is value in having the church doors always open and programs happening daily, as in days of old. That era held significance in terms of the church being a safe place where people of color could come and be validated while finding worth in serving. In many ways, as we collectively face communities of increasing violence and an absence of positive experiences for our youth to be engaged in, the church is again filling that void of a daily safe haven. The challenge for the Hip Hop generation is, how do we ditch the keys and instead of coming to a church building, create those same kinds of safe, holy and validating spaces outside of the church walls? Why can't our cell phones, our computer screens, our cars or local restaurants and bars provide those same kinds of refuge? The answer is that they can, when we create new norms of using technology as a tool for ministry, using local businesses as places to meet and connect and encouraging creative thinking that draws us away from the church and into the community.

APPLICATION

It took a few times before I got it. When we first started Arise, although we streamed all of our worship experiences online, there was an expectation that those who could come to Bible study in-house should do so. So, on Tuesday nights we had a sanctuary full of tired men and women who had worked all day, now trying to quiet their sleepy, tired children so they could hear me rattle off about some Old/New Testament mumbo jumbo. Our Bible studies started at 7pm, and my son's bedtime was at 8pm. Many of the kids who accompanied their parents to Bible Study had similar bedtimes. What we found is that somewhere around 7:30pm **it** would begin. By **it**, I mean the crying, yelling, jumping, slamming...etc. These kids were tired and so were their parents. Our numbers in house steadily declined week after week, while our online numbers remained constant. So, we made a switch! Bible studies would only be offered online, with one night a month offered in-house to meet up and celebrate. Since then, we have seen our online numbers dramatically increase and hear consistent stories of families sitting around the dinner table on Tuesday nights watching bible study, or parents watching from their phones while they fold clothes, clean the house or even take a bath. The point is, if we were going to connect with this generation, we had to make the shift to their worldview.

Group responses to question 5:

What do you hear from those around you regarding their needs in terms of ministry, and in general?

- ✓ We need more children and we need to do more training of ministers
- ✓ Stronger commitment from everyone and a hands on pastor
- ✓ Less judgmental people
- ✓ Practical teaching
- ✓ More fellowship with the believers
- ✓ Powerful encounters with the Lord
- ✓ Someone who cares and will not look down on others
- ✓ Discipleship
- ✓ Someone modeling excellence
- ✓ Less churchy
- ✓ Substance in the sermons
- ✓ To be loved and be accepted without question
- ✓ Intentional Mentorship
- ✓ Simplicity in corporate worship
- ✓ An atmosphere where there can be sharing of issues without being judged
- ✓ Contemporary and political topics addressed with biblical ways of responding to them

Notes Section

In your own personal journey, what could the church have offered you that would have been helpful?

_____

_____

_____

_____

_____

_____

_____

Ask 3 young people what is helpful to them at their churches?

_____

_____

_____

_____

_____

_____

_____

Attraction

(age 33)

"What inspires me is understanding that no matter what challenges I have in life, there is always something inside of me that makes me want to fight for my dreams."

- Dr. Dia LaTrise Liggons

Chapter 6

Attraction

Scripture:
1 Sam 17 31-33

³¹ Now when the words which David spoke were heard, they reported *them* to Saul; and he sent for him. ³² Then David said to Saul, "Let no man's heart fail because of him; your servant will go and fight with this Philistine."

Question:

What attractions do you find in the world but not in the church?

INSIGHT

I took my wife out to a concert one weekend. The act was at a local, small concert hall. We showed up early, had a light dinner across the street from the concert hall, went into the arena, took our seats and watched an amazingly flawless performance. There were well over 50 musicians, dancers and actors coming and going on stage and the entire thing was flawless excellence.

We expected excellence. We expected the staff, the music, the décor, the lighting and even the flow of the performance to be without noticeable hiccups. The Hip Hop generation expects the same thing. Think about it. They watch professional actors on TV, they listen to Grammy- award winning musicians and artists on their radio, and they are surrounded by excellence daily, except when it comes to the church.

When it comes to church, this generation painfully endures out- of - tune pianos, choirs and singers who haven't rehearsed, programs that appear to be pulled together at the last minute, no clear flow, poorly constructed and delivered sermons, …etc. Our churches are not meeting up to the level of excellence that the world offers, and as a result, this generation is becoming less and less interested.

In addition to our lack of excellence, the church is also quickly becoming more exclusive. While many of us are challenged with how to handle social/theological issues, from homosexuality to pluralism, our traditional methods of just throwing rocks at it and calling it sin have only caused a whole generation to push further away. What the Hip Hop generation wrestles with is a society that presents itself as loving and accepting, while the church presents itself as judgmental and exclusive. As a result, it becomes easy to not only dismiss the church as archaic, but also to diminish scripture by labeling it as legalistic.

STRATEGY

1: Invest in Yourself.

Let's get the simple things straight first- microphones, keyboards, sound systems, projectors or screens…etc. Let's look at our order of worship and make sure everyone who is supposed to play a role in worship knows it, has practiced and is ready to go up. Let's have that uncomfortable talk with our musicians and singers about the importance of rehearsing and showing up on time for worship. Let's also look at our facility and make sure it makes sense to guests (you may know where the bathrooms are, but does a visitor?). Lastly, let's get some feedback by recording a worship experience and watching it back with your leadership.

2: Pick Something

Every journey starts with a step. Pick one area of your ministry in which you can focus on becoming excellent. Choose something that your congregation can get excited about. Invite those from the Hip Hop generation to participate in "getting it right." Allow them to take ownership of it, and as a result, watch as it blossoms.

3: Drop the Rocks

There are so many social issues for which the church has no real legitimate answers. Sure, you can piece together a couple of scriptures in order to make a political/theological point, but the reality is that much of the stuff we are faced with in this generation, only God can fix. So our responsibility as believers should be to become ushers, helping people access the presence of God, instead of being bouncers preventing people from entering God's presence simply because we disagree with their lifestyles. The more we lovingly invite people into the presence of God, the more we see those very issues we struggled with, changed.

APPLICATION

After a shooting two blocks away from our church building, we decided to hold a night of prayer. We knew that this would be the first time many in the community would see our facility and so we spent time reorganizing our entrance, sprucing up our welcoming center, labeling our bathrooms, going over our order of worship, putting people in place, and so on. We wanted to make sure our church was ready. During the worship, a member of a different faith asked if he could pray in his faith's language. My response was yes. And so, in the middle of our worship experience, this young man came forward and began chanting in his faith's language. I personally don't know what he was saying, but I do know that by allowing him to be him and providing a space where he could be comfortable, we did more that night in terms of making sustained connections and sharing Jesus than I think has ever been done before in that community.

Group responses to question 6:

What attractions do you find in the world but not in the church?

- ✓ Money, and/or access to resources
- ✓ Youth, the world, sometimes we forget to have fun as Christians
- ✓ People who aren't legalistic
- ✓ Energy
- ✓ Alternative ideas on finding personal peace
- ✓ Excellence in worship
- ✓ A sense of belonging
- ✓ Freedom to be
- ✓ Acceptance
- ✓ A realization that "you are what you are until you change."
- ✓ Freedom to express yourself
- ✓ Offering nonjudgmental support
- ✓ Encouragement

Notes Section

Do you lower your expectations when it comes to church? If so, is that ok?

_____

_____

_____

_____

_____

_____

_____

Ask 3 young people if they feel like they fit in in today's current church culture?

_____

_____

_____

_____

_____

_____

First Steps

(age 26)

"The authentic joy and freedom that I experience in Christ is what inspires me to minister that same hope to others"

-Pastor Carl D Wright

Chapter 7

First Steps

Scripture

Gen 12:1

Now the LORD had said unto Abram, Get thee out of thy country, and from thy kindred, and from thy father's house, unto a land that I will shew thee.

Question:

If the church could fix one thing tomorrow to meet your needs what should it be?

INSIGHT

I love watching renovation shows on TV. It amazes me what difference a fresh coat of paint, new rug, sofa and accent pillows can do to a room. I especially love when there is a budget involved and the homeowners have to make decisions as to what they will invest in and what they will cut. These split second decisions to either cut or keep items have a tremendous effect on how the final product the "reveal" will look.

In many ways ministry is the same thing. If we make a laundry list of all the issues that need addressing in our churches, our programs or teams, that if solved would impact the Hip Hop generation, the list would be overwhelming. The truth is, given our own budgetary constraints and people resources, we are just as limited as some of those renovation shows on TV. So, like them we have to make some decisions regarding what can we do with our current resources now and what can we put off until we are able.

In finance, this mode of operation is called snowballing. Simply put, you start with the easiest, most achievable item/issue and succeed at it, then continue to build momentum and wins by tackling the next smallest issue, continuing this pattern until you have conquered all items and issues.

So, for the Hip Hop generation, what are some easy fixes that can be achieved relatively quickly? The first thing that can be done without much effort is creating welcoming spaces of dialogue. This can be done simply by engaging the Hip Hop generation in intentional conversation. Secondly, as we are engaging in intentional dialogue, we can also redecorate our judgmental stuffy walls with a fresh coat of love and acceptance.

STRATEGY

1: Buy a Vowel

Sometimes you have to gamble a little. It may cost you up front, but it's usually well worth the investment in the end. This principle is true with the Hip Hop generation. Invest time and energy resources into their lives. You will be amazed at the return on your investment. When people know that they are valued and loved, it changes how they respond to the world, and largely, how they see God.

2: Crack Open a Bottle

Sure, there are a number of things that the Hip Hop generation has gotten wrong. Instead of focusing on what is missing, look for areas that you can celebrate, such as education, employment, and entrepreneurial thinking. Celebrate a young adult's passion, encourage them in that area, and you will see growth.

3: Mix it Up

Challenge those in the Hip Hop generation around you to come up with new ideas to existing situations. Enlist them to be a part of developing out-of-the-box, creative solutions.

APPLICATION

When we moved into our first building as a church, I decided that instead of having a traditional ribbon cutting ceremony, we should have an outdoor revival in one of the local parks where we would give away book bags and school supplies to the local community. I met with my team to discuss the idea, and one of our Hip Hop generation members had a different suggestion.

She suggested that instead of a revival, we should do a citywide revival tour where we would set up in different parks throughout the month, doing mini concerts/worship experiences and giving away school supplies with each event. We decided to go with her idea. As a result, in one month we ministered to over 800 people in those 4 weeks, hundreds where prayed for, 43 gave their lives to Christ and countless others connected with our ministry. All of this happened because the one thing we could fix was our ability to listen to and accept fresh ideas.

General Responses to question 7:

If the church could fix one thing tomorrow to meet your needs what should it be?

- ✓ Get rid of the drama
- ✓ Be willing to discuss sexual health of all people
- ✓ Help people value their lives
- ✓ More honesty in dealing with contemporary challenges
- ✓ Unity
- ✓ Preaching that emulates Jesus
- ✓ A worship service planned to intentionally encourage worship
- ✓ Diversity
- ✓ Find better ways to encouraged fellowship
- ✓ More love
- ✓ A support system for single moms
- ✓ An alternative way to give other than with money
- ✓ Better facilities

Notes Section

What will be the immediate first steps you will take to engage young adults, after having read this book?

_____

_____

_____

_____

_____

_____

_____

After having read this book, what young people come to mind that can assist you in answering some of these questions listed?

_____

_____

_____

_____

_____

_____

The Point of it All

Chapter 8:

The Point of it All….

What's the value for me in this book?

As a member of the Hip Hop generation, I see the empty pews. More important than filling these pews, I also see a missing insight. While it is true that this generation of people brings with them a number of issues and baggage, it's also the case that this generation has some needed skill sets that are missing in the church. Ideas like entrepreneurism, marketing, creativity, technological savviness, and boldness are all common to this generation. There is also a freedom that resides in the hearts on today's youth and young adults; a freedom which is valuable to the church. Without them as a significant part of our church communities, as a whole, the church suffers. In short, what this generation brings is not just an energetic presence and income stream, but, ideas, fresh revelations, and concepts that could be overwhelmingly beneficial to the church.

My hope is that as you have read this book, that something within you was triggered to use what you've learned to go after this generation and invite them into dialogue and conversation. In many ways the Hip Hop generation is a generation much like the children of Israel found in the book of Exodus. They are a group of people, creative, free, carrying possibility, but still seeking the promise. Don't be scared of their "different" ideas, but let them in and embrace the change that could change your church, and the world! Value what it is that this generation brings to the table of the Kingdom.. Just remember, it's bigger than Hip Hop!

Appendix A

What is The Arise Church?

Fresh out of Seminary from Regent University, I was hired as Director of Congregational Development and Strengthening the Black Church for the Peninsula Delaware Conference of the United Methodist Church. In April of 2012, while in a routine quarterly meeting with our denominational leadership, our Bishop, then Peggy Johnson, asked me what would be one of the most transformative questions of my entire life. She asked me when I was going to hang a shingle and be at the front end of doing ministry, instead of just consulting with existing ministries. What she could not have known was that my wife and I had been working for over a year on a strategic plan for launching a new faith community. We had been praying and fasting prior to this meeting and we were in position to hear God's clear direction and instruction. This conversation with Bishop Johnson was confirmation Thus, with her "**calling forth**" and support, The Arise Church was born.

My wife and I immediately connected with our partners in ministry: now pastors in their own rights, we shared the vision and began to seek God. It all began at the dinner table with a launch team of four people; two married couples, and our four children, total. Soon after, two other young married couples joined us at the dinner table of planning, brainstorming, fasting, and praying. With that, The Arise Church started in the fellowship hall of an existing United Methodist Church, meeting on Tuesday and Friday nights. In less than one year, the ministry grew from **8 people to over 200** in weekly worship attendance, including Bible Study, Fresh Friday Service, Sunday Morning Worship, and online viewers. Once we added a Sunday morning worship service, we moved locations and expanded in ministry opportunities. We knew early on, that our vision was too big for a fellowship hall, but we had to start somewhere.

We quickly began to see that the culture of our church was appealing to young adults, and people who wanted something different. The people who came to Arise and <u>remained</u> were looking for relationship, NOT RELIGION. Here is a bit of insight on how why we have been successful.

- ✓ We **communicate and share the vision**, which is to LOVE and EMPOWER, constantly, and consistently, in everything that we do at Arise. Every chance we get, we talk about the vision and what it truly means. This allows everyone to be aligned with the vision. When everyone knows the vision, they can run with it. All ministries and events are planned around loving and empowering ALL people.
- ✓ My wife and I are young at heart, and we have an **urban flare** that attracts young adults. Because my family did not have a specific dress code, people felt comfortable in either a dress or suit, or jeans and tennis shoes. This created a true "come as you are" atmosphere. The presence of our two year old son allowed other families to be comfortable with their kids moving around and about. For young families, this is a plus.
- ✓ We immediately created a **youth ministry**, and we worked with the youth during every service, regardless of how many showed up. This created an atmosphere for the family. When parents know that their children are being taken care of, they are more likely to come to church with their children. For many parents, church is a "break" for them.
- ✓ We live streamed every **service online**, from day one, allowing curious people and family and friends to tune in to see what the Arise buzz is all about. Several of our members are a result of our online streaming.
- ✓ There is no program given to people as they walk in, but our members and **hospitality** team greet and love every single person who comes in the doors. This promotes personal communications and connections between the people, as opposed to communication through paper. The personal touches mean a lot to people.

- ✓ Visitor **follow up** is a crucial part of what people look for, today. People want to know that they are valued, so we make a conscious effort to reach out to them within one week of them visiting the church.
- ✓ The order of service is **free flowing**. We have a plan, but God's plan always overrules. We follow where the Holy Spirit leads, and because of this, we see signs, wonders, and miracles take place each week because of the freedom in the atmosphere.
- ✓ The **worship atmosphere** is one of freedom and liberty. If people want to shout, sing, dance, run, or sit silently in God's presence, we welcome it. We want people of different backgrounds, cultures, and ethnicities to be free to express in the way they choose.
- ✓ The **music is diverse**, with a mix of hymns, contemporary Christian music, Gospel music, and many times, a soul and jazz flare. We do this, so that all kinds of people can relate to the worship experience. We also integrate the arts, such as prophetic painting, dance, and poetry, which attracts the hip hop generation.
- ✓ We aren't afraid to **try new things**. If a member has an idea, our first response is of course to pray, but if their idea is aligned with our vision to "love" and "empower", we immediately link them with someone who can support and help bring the vision to pass. For example, we reached over 400 people, outside of the church when we did a Trunk or Treat on Halloween. We couldn't be scared to try what others wouldn't. We reached the people with the message of Christ and His love on Halloween night.

Arise is a multi-ethnic multi-lingual congregation, welcoming all. This community is deeply committed to meeting people where they are and so the church has both an **intentional** online presence: offering online bible studies, book series and other internet ministries, as well as a **radical** community presence.

Arise is committed to five key areas: **Revolutionary Spiritual Growth, Reclaiming the Arts, Restoring the Family, Relevant Education and Radical Evangelism.** Our core beliefs can be summed up in one word: **Love.** We believe that God's love triumphs everything. We believe that healing and wholeness happen in the presence of God's love. We believe that all things work together for the good of those who love God. We believe that all were created through love with purpose and that only through accepting the love of Christ can that purpose be fully understood. Lastly, we believe that its God's love that connects us to each other and holds us responsible for our brothers and sisters.

Appendix B

AUTHOR'S BIO

Ron serves as one of the founders and lead pastor of the Arise Church. Ron's passion is helping people uncover their destiny and find/renew their relationship with Jesus Christ. Ron is married to Dr. Eboni M. Bell and the couple has one awesome son, Ronald Bell, III. Pastor Ron is committed to three things: empowering and loving everyone he comes into contact with, practical teaching of the Word of God, and helping others discover their purpose and destiny in life.

Ron is a creative soul, a musician, and a nationally recognized new church start consultant and a coach. He is also an entrepreneur, and has a company, Belle Bowties. Pastor Ron has also served as Director of Congregational Development and SBC21 for the Peninsula Delaware United Methodist Conference. In addition to full time pastoring, writing and coaching, Pastor Ron also serves currently as a national associate for Path 1. Ron is passionate about seeing people grow in Christ, and fighting for social justice issues. Ron has also authored several articles and ministry resources.

Ron is currently completing his Doctorate in Theology (D.Min) from Lancaster Theological Seminary; he has a Masters in Theology (MA) from Regent University and a Bachelor's in Philosophy (BA) from Morgan State University. Ron serves on several boards and agencies, and is both certified and licensed to pastor by the United Methodist Church.

For more information of the author, and other resources and products, visit **www.RonaldBellJr.com**, or contact him at ronaldbelljr@gmail.com.

Acknowledgments

Cover Art and Layout:	Strikingly Odd Productions
Editing:	Dorothy Ann Jackson/Eboni Bell
Interior Pictures:	Okey Nwaneri
	Travis Dunlap
	Eboni M Bell
	Hannah Bonner
	Dia LaTrise Liggons
	Carl D Wright
Photo Design:	Ta'Tra Bradshaw Brown
	Anya Elizabeth Tape
Support:	Travis Smith/Russell Delegation/nbmuzica
	Peninsula-Delaware Conference UMC
	Team Bell

The Arise Movement!!!!!

CHRISTIAN HIP HOP MEETS CHOIR WITH REMAKE OF AL B SURE CLASSIC

GET YOUR FREE MUSIC DOWNLOAD TODAY
WWW.BIGGERTHANHIPHOP.COM

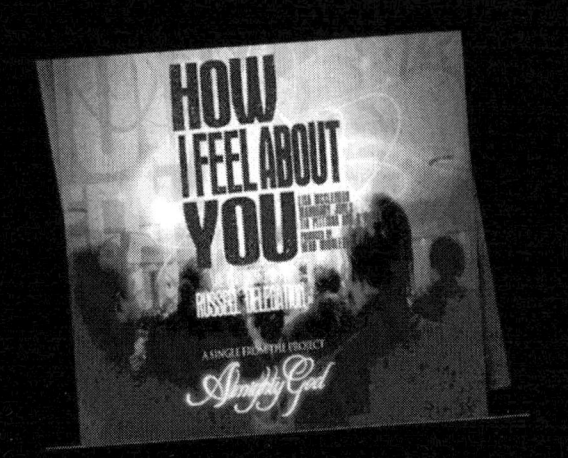

RUSSELL DELEGATION
featuring
Lisa McClendon Mahogany Jones Tia Pittman B'Wellz

From The Project *Almighty God*

nbmuzica

Made in the USA
Charleston, SC
02 July 2014